OPPOSITE: ROBBEN ISLAND AND THE MAGNIFICENT BACKDROP OF TABLE MOUNTAIN. **ABOVE:** THE ENTRANCE TO THE ISLAND DATES BACK TO WHEN IT WAS A MAXIMUM SECURITY PRISON.

FOR 400 YEARS, FROM ITS BEGINNINGS AS A DUMPING GROUND FOR MUTINEERS UP UNTIL ITS MODERN LIFE AS A MUSEUM, ROBBEN ISLAND HAS BEEN A SYMBOL OF OPPRESSION AND PUNISHMENT.

Among the unhappy inhabitants incarcerated on this flat and windswept island were slaves, Khoikhoi and African leaders, lepers, the mentally ill and, most recently, anti-apartheid freedom fighters, including the likes of Nelson Mandela, Walter Sisulu and Govan Mbeki. Since the end of apartheid in 1994 Robben Island or 'Esiqithini', as it is known in Xhosa, has become a World Heritage Site, a museum, and an international symbol of freedom and human rights.

FERRY TO THE ISLAND

For the many thousands of tourists who visit the Island each year, the journey begins at the Nelson Mandela Gateway to Robben Island, situated in the heart of Cape Town's famous Victoria & Alfred Waterfront.

At the Gateway you can purchase books about the Island, as well as memorabilia, and you can enjoy the fascinating exhibits on display in the museum. The 11-kilometre ferry trip to the Island takes roughly 30 minutes if you are booked aboard the modern *Makana* or *Autshumato*, and slightly longer if you are on one of the historic ferries. On the way out of the docks, be prepared for the dramatic view of Table Bay, Cape Town and Table Mountain. From August to December, southern right whales come to calve in the bay and there are often seals to be seen. In fact, the Island gets its name from the Dutch word for seal.

ABOVE: THE NELSON MANDELA GATEWAY IS BESIDE THE CLOCK TOWER IN THE VICTORIA & ALFRED WATERFRONT.

RIGHT: THE *MAKANA* DEPARTS FOR THE ISLAND.

LEFT: VIEWS OF TABLE MOUNTAIN FROM ONE OF THE HISTORIC FERRIES, WHICH HAVE BEEN IN SERVICE SINCE THE 1960s. **BELOW:** THE FERRY ARRIVES AT MURRAY'S BAY HARBOUR.

RIGHT: VISITORS TO THE ISLAND ARE MET BY GUIDES, AND WILL CONTINUE THEIR TOUR OF THE ISLAND PARTLY BY BUS, AND PARTLY ON FOOT THROUGH THE PRISON.

EARLY HISTORY

ROBBEN ISLAND, WHICH IS 12 KILOMETRES IN CIRCUMFERENCE, WAS A CONVENIENT PLACE FOR SAILORS TO HUNT FOR PENGUINS, SEALS AND TORTOISES ON THEIR WAY AROUND THE CAPE.

After 1652, when the Dutch colonialists established a permanent base in the Cape, they used it as a source of food, and of lime and slate for their buildings. Jan van Riebeeck found the Island a convenient place to put anyone who threatened the colonial order, including his Khoikhoi interpreter Autshumato and later Autshumato's niece Krotoa. In the

centuries that followed, slaves from various parts of Africa and Asia were dumped here, as well as political and religious Muslim leaders who opposed Dutch colonialism in East Africa. The British continued this tradition in the 1800s by putting their political prisoners on the Island, including various Xhosa chiefs who resisted colonial expansion.

OPPOSITE TOP, AND LEFT: AN 1868 LINOCUT AND AN EARLY PHOTOGRAPH SHOW XHOSA CHIEFS IMPRISONED ON THE ISLAND. **OPPOSITE LEFT:** KROTOA WAS A FAVOURITE SERVANT IN THE VAN RIEBEECK HOUSEHOLD AND LATER MARRIED A DUTCH DOCTOR. SHE WAS MALIGNED BY DUTCH SOCIETY AFTER HIS DEATH AND BANISHED TO THE ISLAND. **ABOVE:** IN THE 1800s THERE WAS NO HARBOUR, AND CONVICTS CARRIED PASSENGERS AND CARGO TO THEIR SHIPS.

LEFT: THE DORMITORY FOR THE WHITE LEPERS BEING BURNT DOWN IN THE 1930s.

ABOVE: A RACIST COMPARISON BETWEEN A MENTALLY ILL PATIENT AND A BABOON.

FROM 1846 TO 1931 ROBBEN ISLAND ACCOMMODATED MEDICAL FACILITIES, INCLUDING A HOSPITAL FOR MENTALLY ILL PEOPLE, LEPERS AND THE CHRONICALLY SICK.

During the 1800s patients lived in appalling conditions, and there are terrible stories of rape and ill treatment. The law at

SOCIETY'S OUTCASTS

that time stipulated that lepers were not permitted to live in normal society, so hundreds of them were shipped to the Island, where they stayed in virtual isolation for up to 50 years. In the early 1900s care improved, and by the 1930s lepers and mentally ill patients were integrated into mainland hospitals.

LEFT: THE LEPER GRAVEYARD. **ABOVE:** A MUSICAL BAND FORMED BY LEPROSY SUFFERERS. **BELOW:** FEMALE LEPERS PREPARING THEIR FOOD IN THE EARLY 20TH CENTURY.

OVER THE CENTURIES AT LEAST 29 SHIPS HAVE BEEN WRECKED OFF ROBBEN ISLAND – AND THERE ARE STRANGE TALES APLENTY.

There's the story of the phantom *Flying Dutchman*, with its sails in tatters, which mariners said could sometimes be seen here during the furious Cape storms. Originally, fires were lit at the top of Minto Hill, the highest point on the Island, to warn ships, but they were replaced by the present lighthouse, which was built in 1864. Only a few prisoners attempted to escape through the rough

SHIPWRECKS AND ESCAPES

OPPOSITE TOP: THE BRITISH LINER *RANGATIRA* WAS WRECKED IN A STORM IN 1916. **OPPOSITE BOTTOM, AND RIGHT:** SEVERAL TAIWANESE FISHING TRAWLERS HAVE FOUNDERED HERE IN RECENT YEARS. **BELOW:** PLAATJIES, A MENTAL PATIENT, MADE SEVERAL ESCAPE VESSELS, ALL OF WHICH WERE DESTROYED BY ORDERLIES.

seas surrounding the Island. In 1819, the Xhosa leader and prophet Makana, imprisoned for leading an attack on the colonialists at Grahamstown, and 30 others made for shore in a whaler's longboat. They foundered on the rocks at Blouberg, where Makana drowned.

WORLD WAR II

During World War II, Robben Island was fortified by the Allies in order to protect the sea route around the southern tip of Africa. To make the port 'battleship proof', they also built Murray's Bay harbour, an airfield, several large gun batteries, as well as extensive dormitories for troops. It was the only place in South Africa where women and black Cape Corps soldiers were

ABOVE: MEMBERS OF THE WOMEN'S AUXILIARY AIR FORCE (WAAF) IN THE PLOTTING ROOM ON ROBBEN ISLAND. **RIGHT:** ONE OF TWO ENORMOUS 9,2-INCH GUN BATTERIES, WHICH WERE PLACED ON ROBBEN ISLAND DURING THE WAR.

trained for combat. The school's enormous battery of guns was never fired in anger, but it is said that, when fired once during a training session, they made a thundering sound and their flames set alight some of the Island's gum trees.

ABOVE: SUBMARINE DETECTION CABLES STRETCHED FROM ROBBEN ISLAND TO THE MAINLAND. TWO SHIPS WERE TORPEDOED BY U-BOATS WITHIN 40 KILOMETRES OF CAPE TOWN. **RIGHT:** WAAF ARTILLERY SPECIALISTS LEAVING THE GUNNERY SCHOOL ON ROBBEN ISLAND.

ABOVE: THE MAXIMUM SECURITY COMPLEX WAS COMPLETED IN 1964. **RIGHT:** FROM THE SENTRY TOWER WARDENS KEPT A CONSTANT WATCH OVER THE PRISON.

POLITICAL PRISON

IN 1948 THE NATIONAL PARTY GOVERNMENT CAME TO POWER, THEIR HARSH APARTHEID POLICIES WORSENING EXISTING RACIAL DISCRIMINATION.

They attempted to suppress opposition by banning the African National Congress (ANC) and the Pan-Africanist Congress (PAC) in 1960. South African Prison Services took over the Island on 1 April 1961 mainly for non-political prisoners, but as the apartheid clampdown intensified it became a high-security prison for the political activists. In June 1964, after the famous Rivonia Trial, senior ANC members, including Nelson Mandela, Walter Sisulu, Govan Mbeki and Ahmed Kathrada, were sentenced to life imprisonment on the Island.

ABOVE AND RIGHT: VISITORS TO ROBBEN ISLAND MUSEUM ENCOUNTER THE HARSH REALITIES OF THE PRISON'S HISTORY. **TOP RIGHT:** A PRISONER'S VIEW OF THE MAXIMUM SECURITY COMPLEX.

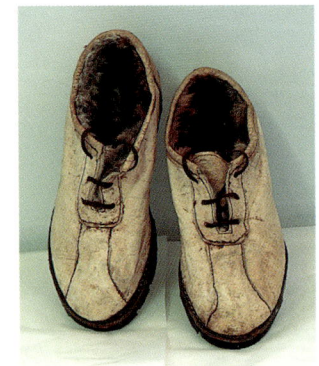

During the 1960s and '70s the maximum security prison on Robben Island was known as the 'hell-hole' of apartheid and became notorious for its brutal and spartan conditions. The idea was to crush government opponents and the ideas they stood for. But the freedom fighters remained resolute: 'Improve your education and be prepared to govern,' Nelson Mandela told his fellow prisoners. They gave lectures on a variety of subjects, from ANC strategy to anthropology, and many prisoners went on to earn degrees. Meanwhile, the unified call for the release of Nelson Mandela and the other prisoners on Robben Island could be heard throughout the world.

TOP LEFT: A GALLERY OF COMMANDING OFFICERS. **TOP RIGHT:** SHOES MADE BY PRISONER BABA MDLALOSE FOR FELLOW PRISONER SAZI VEDLTMAN, WHO SUFFERED FROM ARTHRITIS. **ABOVE:** PRISONERS MET THEIR LAWYERS IN THIS ROOM. **LEFT:** IN THE 1960s PAC LEADER ROBERT SOBUKWE WAS IN SOLITARY CONFINEMENT IN THIS SMALL HOUSE.

ABOVE: PRISONERS, IN THE 1960s, IN THE PRISON COURTYARD BREAKING ROCKS AND SEWING MAILBAGS. **RIGHT:** NELSON MANDELA'S OLD PRISON CELL, AS IT LOOKS TODAY.

LEFT: NELSON MANDELA TALKS TO HIS FELLOW RIVONIA TRIALIST WALTER SISULU, IN THE PRISON COURTYARD. THEY ARE WEARING WARM CLOTHES PROVIDED FOR THE PRESS'S VISIT AND TAKEN AWAY AFTERWARDS.

ABOVE: AHMED KATHRADA CELEBRATING HIS RELEASE. **RIGHT:** THE PRISON FENCES LEFT BEHIND. **BELOW:** MANY PRISONERS DONATED THEIR POSSESSIONS TO THE MAYIBUYE CENTRE (NOW PART OF THE ROBBEN ISLAND MUSEUM) AND THESE BECAME KNOWN AS THE APPLE BOX ARCHIVES.

FREE AT LAST

LEFT: EX-PRISONERS (LEFT TO RIGHT) RAYMOND MHLABA, OSCAR MPETHA, ANDREW MLANGENI, WALTER SISULU, AHMED KATHRADA, ELIAS MOTSOALEDI AND WILTON MKWAYI SHORTLY AFTER THEIR RELEASE IN 1989. **BELOW:** NELSON MANDELA, HIS WIFE GRAÇA MACHEL, AND CHRISTO BRAND, A FORMER PRISON WARDER AND A FRIEND OF MANDELA.

VARIOUS NATIONAL PARTY DELEGATIONS TRIED TO PERSUADE THE POLITICAL PRISONERS TO ACCEPT SOME FORM OF APARTHEID GOVERNMENT AND TO DENOUNCE THE ANC PUBLICLY.

'I am not prepared to sell the birthright of my people to be free,' replied Nelson Mandela, summing up the view of all the prisoners. International isolation was bankrupting the country and, by the late 1980s, the release of political prisoners began. By February 1990 the ANC and the PAC had been unbanned, and Mandela and the Rivonia trialists were free. Four years later the ANC came to power in South Africa's first democratic elections and Mandela became president.

On 11 February 1995 – the fifth anniversary of Mandela's release from prison – more than 1,000 ex-prisoners, as well as the media, set sail aboard the SAS *Outeniqua* for an historic reunion on the Island.

On this day ex-political prisoners returned to Robben Island for the first time as free people, and a symbolic rock-breaking ceremony was held in the lime quarry where they had worked while incarcerated. 'Never again shall South Africa imprison its citizens simply because they disagree with the government of the day,' said Nelson Mandela in his address.

ABOVE: NELSON MANDELA REVISITS HIS OLD PRISON CELL AND LOOKS OUT FROM THE TINY ROOM HE LIVED IN FOR SO MANY YEARS.

RIGHT: MANDELA GREETS A PRISON WARDER.

RETURNING TO THE ISLAND

OPPOSITE TOP: THE HISTORIC ROCK-BREAKING CEREMONY WAS HELD IN THE LIME QUARRY WHERE THE PRISONERS HAD BEEN FORCED TO WORK IN THE BAKING SUN. **LEFT:** AFTERWARDS THE EX-PRISONERS EACH PLACED A STONE TO BUILD THIS SYMBOLIC CAIRN. **BELOW:** THE RIVONIA TRIALISTS, (LEFT TO RIGHT) DENNIS GOLDBERG, ANDREW MLANGENI, NELSON MANDELA, AHMED KATHRADA AND WALTER SISULU, IN THE LIME QUARRY.

ROBBEN ISLAND WAS OPENED TO THE PUBLIC ON 1 JANUARY 1997 AND WAS DECLARED A UNESCO WORLD HERITAGE SITE IN DECEMBER 1999.

Professor André Odendaal, of the Mayibuye Centre, and a team of workers were appointed to create an on-site museum, which would deal with education, tourism and conservation. The core focus, though, would be the Island's recent political history and its important message of freedom, human rights and democracy.

THE ISLAND TODAY

The curators took great care to preserve Robben Island's complex layers of culture, religion and history, which are revealed through its fascinating landscape, wildlife and architecture. The museum, which hosts regular conferences and also runs a wide range of programmes for school children and community groups, provides a cultural showcase for the country's new democracy.

OPPOSITE TOP: AN AERIAL VIEW. **OPPOSITE BOTTOM, AND LEFT:** PLACES OF WORSHIP INCLUDE THE ANGLICAN CHURCH (1841) AND THE KRAMAT (1969), ERECTED OVER THE GRAVE OF SAYED ADUROHMAN MONTURU, PRINCE OF MADEIRA, WHO DIED HERE IN 1754. **ABOVE:** THE GUEST HOUSE, THE OLD GOVERNOR'S RESIDENCE, DATES BACK TO THE 1890s.

23

THE LAST PRISONERS AND WARDERS LEFT IN EARLY 1997 AND SINCE THEN A NEW COMMUNITY HAS DEVELOPED.

The Island has approximately 150 permanent residents, including ex-prisoners and ex-warders, who staff the Robben Island Museum and other facilities. Running the Island's tourism and educational facilities is difficult, though, as everything has to come in by ship. And, with no fresh water, they have to desalinate seawater to drink. Services on the Island include a workshop and garage, modern offices, a restaurant, as well as conference and guest facilities. There are churches catering for several denominations, and a junior school attended by some 40 children. A number of mainlanders commute to and from the Island daily (and some islanders commute to the mainland).

TOP LEFT: ROBBEN ISLAND'S MAIN STREET WITH THE ANGLICAN CHURCH IN THE BACKGROUND. **LEFT:** CHARLÉ NEL FRANKS THE MAIL AT THE ROBBEN ISLAND POST OFFICE. **OPPOSITE BOTTOM LEFT:** EX-WARDER FRIKKIE NEL WITH THE ROBBEN ISLAND AMBULANCE..

ISLANDERS AT WORK

OPPOSITE TOP RIGHT: EX-WARDER CHRISTO BRAND GIVES SHOPPING ADVICE AT THE NELSON MANDELA GATEWAY BOOKSHOP.

RIGHT AND BOTTOM RIGHT: THE VITAL JOB OF KEEPING SHIPS OFF THE ROCKS IS UP TO MERVYN WHITE, WHO RUNS THE LIGHTHOUSE.

BELOW: JANNETTE BAXTER WORKS IN THE ROBBEN ISLAND SHOP.

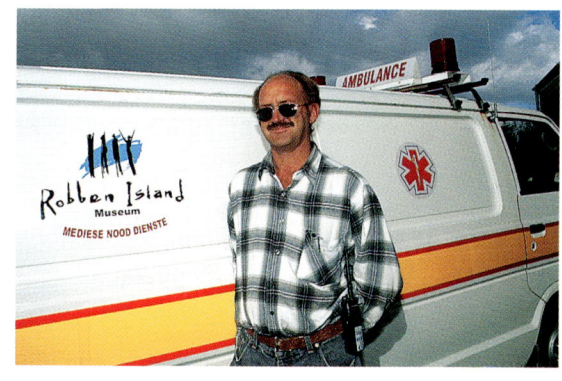

ISLAND LIFE

ABOVE: ROBBEN JUNIOR ISLAND SCHOOL. **TOP:** MEDIA OFFICER ESTHER HENDERSON AND HER FAMILY ARE PERMANENT RESIDENTS. **RIGHT:** FREE AT LAST! SCHOOL IS FINISHED FOR THE DAY.

When the last of the many tourist ferries has returned to the mainland, Island residents settle down for the night.

For the first time in 400 years the Island is free and peaceful. As the sun sets over the sea and the gulls roost for the night, you will find families sitting down for dinner and parents putting their children to bed. Robben Island's residents are as fascinating as the history of the Island, and if you take a walk to the old canteen you can see ex-prisoners and ex-warders sharing a drink in an atmosphere of reconciliation and respect.

ABOVE: A TYPICAL ISLAND RESIDENCE, DATING BACK OVER A CENTURY. **LEFT:** EX-POLITICAL PRISONER, GUIDE AND ARTIST LIONEL DAVIS (LEFT) RELAXING AT THE END OF THE DAY WITH A FELLOW RESIDENT.

ISLAND FLORA AND FAUNA

Don't be surprised to see herds of fallow deer on Robben Island. Along with a number of other species of antelope, these animals were originally introduced for sport hunting  and may be seen grazing next to indigenous eland, steenbok, bontebok and springbok.

European rabbits were brought to the Island by Van Riebeeck in 1654 as a source of food, and their descendants are now extremely numerous. Wattle, bluegum, pine, cyprus and manitoka trees were introduced to Robben Island between 1892 and 1912 to give some shelter to the lepers who were left suffering on the Island.

ABOVE: AN OLD PHOTOGRAPH OF THE ISLAND'S ARUM LILIES FLOWERING AFTER THE RAINS. **BELOW:** WATERFOWL CONGREGATE IN THE POOLS AT VAN RIEBEECK'S QUARRY.

OPPOSITE TOP LEFT. CHUKAR PARTRIDGE BREED NOWHERE ELSE IN SOUTH AFRICA. **OPPOSITE TOP RIGHT:** AN ANGULATE TORTOISE. **OPPOSITE BOTTOM:** BONTEBOK ARE RARE ELSEWHERE IN SOUTH AFRICA. **ABOVE:** MOLE SNAKES FEED ON EGGS.

THE ISLAND COAST

Robben Island is fringed by a marine sanctuary where perlemoen, crayfish and other sea life are protected: no harvesting is permitted.

The Island has more than 70 species of bird. Many, such as the African black oystercatcher, African penguin, Damara tern and bank cormorant, are endangered and protected. African penguins, displaced from the Island after extensive exploitation, began to return in 1993. Their Robben Island colony, now consisting of nearly 20,000 birds, is the third largest in the world for this species.

OPPOSITE TOP LEFT: A PAIR OF OYSTERCATCHERS GUARD THEIR NEST. **OPPOSITE BOTTOM:** ALPHA ONE, WHICH WAS A BAR DURING PRISON TIMES, IS SITUATED RIGHT ON THE ROCKS. **LEFT:** AFRICAN PENGUINS, WHICH NEST BY THE THOUSANDS ON THE ISLAND'S EASTERN SHORES, CAN BE VIEWED FROM A HIDE AND A WOODEN BOARDWALK.

ABOVE: THOUSANDS OF CORMORANTS MAKE THEIR NESTS ON THE HARBOUR WALL. **LEFT:** BANK CORMORANTS, WHICH BREED IN ONLY A FEW SITES IN SOUTH AFRICA, ARE AN ATTRACTION FOR BIRDERS.

ABOVE: THE VICTORIA & ALFRED WATERFRONT, SEEN FROM THE NELSON MANDELA GATEWAY CENTRE. **OPPOSITE:** A VIEW OF ROBBEN ISLAND FROM SIGNAL HILL, ON THE MAINLAND.

First published in 2002 by Struik Publishers and the Robben Island Museum
(a division of New Holland Publishing (South Africa) (Pty) Ltd)
London • Cape Town • Sydney • Auckland

Garfield House
86–88 Edgware Road
W2 2EA London
United Kingdom
www.newhollandpublishers.com

80 McKenzie Street
Cape Town
8001
South Africa
www.struik.co.za

14 Aquatic Drive
Frenchs Forest, NSW 2086
Australia

218 Lake Road
Northcote, Auckland
New Zealand

New Holland Publishing is a member of the Johnnic Publishing Group

ISBN 1 86872 785 8

10 9 8 7 6 5 4 3 2 1

Log on to our photographic website
www.imagesofafrica.co.za for an African experience.

www.robben-island.org.za

Picture Credits: CA: Cape Archives; DDP: DD Photography; DR: David Rogers; EM: Eric Miller; HvH: Hein von Hörsten; IA: IAfrika; JS: Jürgen Shadeberg; LG: Louise Gubb; LH: Leonard Hoffmann; MA: Mayibuye Archives; MH: Mike Hutchings; MHH: M H Hill; NL: National Library; NMS: Naval Museum, Simonstown; PWL: PW Laidler; RdlH: Roger de la Harpe; RIM: Robben Island Museum; SA: Shaen Adey; SIL: Struik Image Library; TI: Trace Images; UWC: University of the Western Cape

Copyright © 2002 in photographs: as listed below

Front cover: (pics 1–8, clockwise from top left) 1: SA/SIL, 2: DR, 3: UWC/RIM/MA, 4: SA/SIL, 5: HvH/SIL, 6: JS, 7 & 8: SA/SIL; **Inside front cover:** DR; **Page 1:** SA/SIL; **2:** (both) DR; **3:** (top) SA/SIL, (middle) DR, (bottom) SA/SIL; **4:** (top) NL, (bottom left) PWL, (bottom right) NL; **5:** NL; **6:** (left and top right) NL, (bottom right) DR; **7:** (both) CA; **8:** (top) NL, (bottom) DR; **9:** (top) DR, (bottom) NL; **10:** (top) MHH/NL, (bottom) DR; **11:** (top) NMS, (bottom) MHH/NL; **12, 13 and 14:** (all) DR; **15:** (top and bottom left) UWC/RIM/MA, (middle right) DR; **18:** (top left) EM/IA, (top right) DR, (bottom) MH; **19:** (top) EM/IA, (bottom) Christo Brand; **20:** (top) UWC/RIM/MA, (middle and bottom) LG/TI; **21:** (top) SA/SIL, (bottom) JS; **22:** (top) DR, (bottom) SA/SIL; **23:** (top) HvH/SIL, (bottom) DR; **24:** (top left) SA/SIL, (top right, centre and bottom) DR; **25:** (top right and bottom left) DR, (bottom right) HvH/SIL; **26:** (top) SA/SIL, (top right, middle and bottom) DR; **27:** (top) SA/SIL, (bottom) DR; **28:** (top left) DR, (top right and bottom) RdlH/DDP; **29:** (top) NL, (middle) LH/SIL, (bottom) HvH/SIL; **30 and 31:** (all) DR; **32:** DR; **Inside back cover:** SA/SIL; **Back cover:** pics 1–8, clockwise from top left) 1: DR, 2: NL, 3: SA/SIL, 4 & 5: DR, 6: RIM, 7 & 8: DR

Front cover, clockwise from top left: The entrance to Robben Island; an aerial view of the Island; political prisoners breaking rocks and sewing mailbags; tourists disembarking from the ferry; the old Governor's residence, now a guest house; Mandela revisting his old cell as a free man; a symbolic cairn made by ex-prisoners; the Robben Island lighthouse on Minto Hill.

Back cover, clockwise from top left: A bontebok grazing; Xhosa chiefs incarcerated on the Island; visitors admiring the view of Table Mountain from Robben Island; a deserted hallway in the maximum security prison; some of the island's thousands of African penguins; the Robben Island Museum logo; a wrecked Taiwanese fishing trawler; the Island Kramat.

Publishing manager: Annlerie van Rooyen
Managing editor: Lesley Hay-Whitton
Design director: Janice Evans
Concept design: Michelle Ludek
Designer: Alison Day
Editor: Monique Whitaker
Picture researcher: Carmen Watts
Cartographer: Anthony Riley

Copyright © 2002 in published edition: Struik Publishers
Copyright © 2002 in text: David Rogers
Copyright © 2002 in map on page 16–17: Struik Publishers

Reproduction by Hirt & Carter Cape (Pty) Ltd
Printed by Craft Print Pte Ltd

All rights reserved. No part of this publication may be reproduced, stored in a retrieval system or transmitted, in any form or by any means, electronic, mechanical, photocopying or otherwise, without the prior written permission of the publishers and copyright holders.